The Pomong U'tau of Dreams: a collection of Bougainvillean poetry

Leonard Fong Roka

Pukpuk Publications

The Pomong U'tau of Dreams

ISBN: 978-0-9871321-4-7

DEDICATION

For my family members of hamlets Kavarongnau, Mak'osi, Kaspeke (Œvo-Torau) and Unang in the Panguna District of Bougainville

And relatives of Manopo Village in Bali Island of West New Britain Province of Papua New Guinea; and to my many friends in every corner of the Pacific that I have met in one part of my life.

CONTENTS

The Pomong U'tau of Dreams

ACKNOWLEDGMENTS

This collection would not have been what it is without the help and suggestions of the various Bougainvilleans I encounter in my daily life: my uncle, Robert Perakai in Elutupan village on Buka Island; my kinsmen of Tumpusiong valley in the Panguna district; and those mountain people, in Kupe village of the North Nasioi District

INTRODUCTION

Every human being on Earth encounters different things in their lifetime. We talk about them to our friends and family because we are natural story tellers, just like our progenitors. For generations we have passed down oral history and are still doing it now.

The introduction of writing turned the stories into objects that you can touch, look at, and store. The written word today is also a tool that enables the writer to record and save from change or distortion those artistic values in stories and poetry that might otherwise lose their sacred meaning and degrade their literary value and purpose for Melanesian society.

Part of the writer's job is to educate and bring about changes to society, as I am attempting to do for my people of Bougainville, who have long being subjugated by outsiders.

The Pomong Utau of Dreams is a collection of poetry consisting of my leisure time writing since 1997. In it I try to frankly celebrate all aspects of Bougainville culture: politics, anthropology, sociology, history and even my own personal experiences in life. It is you, the reader, who I hope will learn and get pleasure out of the poems.

The poem, *My Panguna*, was my very first. I wrote it for the 1997 Arawa High School Jubilee Magazine but it was not accepted for publication.

Poems for the Beauty of our
LAND

My Beloved Country

Living in Bougainville is joy
like giving birth…
Listening to her singing voice
liberates off slavery
like Moses the Jew…
Lying on a fine beach with her
lipping me all over
lights the world anew
like rain that waters to life the land…
Loving her lucids my mind, so
leaving her is a heart break
like sudden divorce….

Domena

Mystic candle light
A stare clears my eye's dirt
Restarts all new life

Beach Wonder

What are sands?
Those trillions on the beach?
On the shore they lie
Innocent they seem
Smarter than the night sky they sing.
But yet those angry waves
Punish that embrace of peace to funny agony….
And now the sky seem a beauty
In harmony above
My gloomy head,
Papa.

Takuang

Menacingly tall
Knapsacks streams of salty sweat
Oh, peak of glories

Lone Mountain Palm

Strike by the wind's tentacles
O'er and o'er and
O'er again
You kneel to
Weeping
Polished
Relegated
Fruitless, oh
Swaying sorrow

Kara

Erotic pillow
Keeps me sailing the oceans
Those warmest lickings

The Ioro Country Song

My Kokore
Is a fecund mountain
And that hoodwinking humming Guava
Docks in delicately like dove – tail
As hungry Moroni and Dapera

Do-done!
Eyeing Enamira and Damara
In the near distance
Where the cry of hornbills is no-more
Hides Desike, deep, somewhere
Beside teary one, Onove
As Enamira and Damara
Play them the awesome tunes
Of refreshing Kavarong.

But why, Mosinau
And daringly dating Poaru
And that knead-longing Pangka
Sit silently and stare
Into the azure expanse?
Do they admire, Orami?
Go on
My great Enamira …
To the beautiful songs of
Pinenari

Kake

Humble servant
Lend my wife that warmth
Peaceful heart
Moon

The Kieta Song

Eyes from the peaks and clouds
Fall astray in pure wonder,
Of great hills and valleys
Canonized by myths and legends

Of mysterious deeds and courage.

O women of the feasting nights
Mungkasize my breath with tamatama
Stain my lips with magic coconut oil
Breathing secular dreams and wonders

O girls of oily skin and
Odorous herbs of the feasting nights-
The alarm of joy to drowning norms and taboos-
Cherish my zeal of siriroi
With waving of arms and biriko
And singing of mystic verses
Celebrating the ancestral deeds
Whilst on earthly sojourns.

O dancer of the spirited giddiness,
Keep the divinity of your steps chaste
With smell of pork and herbs;
The powers tangled to reaping of taro plots
For men and children
With wigs of learning

O dancers of the cremation nights
Mungkasize my loins
With spirited torches restarting the world.
Hand me the flute of magic
Homaging the soul of the death
With new tempos of heavenly saneness
Pouring in from the thousand coloured flames;
That apparition of spirits
From the hills and valleys,
E, gods of taro and yams.

O masters of harvest of fruitions
Rise o'er the black dancer
Inspire him, child of the unseen
Heroes of legends

O menfolk of the marriage nights
Mungkasize my spirits
With erotic ode and siriroi
Cast the shadow of your naked jubiliation
Upon my desperate spirit
Paint my heart with dramas of marriage
Before the tamatama
And my face smeared with those oils
Erupting the powers of vision
To dawn like morning on the tora of taro
For the night's art to share.

O women of crimson lips
With areca nuts and gingers
Spit on my palm that power…
That blood of oneness in two clans
Waking the loins of women
To mould the world and spirits.

O women, spit on the garden's
Yams and taro. The
Banana and pork under the hot stones,
Spit, o women, spit
On my bare chest…
Kindle the fires of learning
Smear upon the clans
The odour of heirship,
O dancers.

The Perfect Road

Evergreen smile:
Pure, humble and chaste.
Those clouds that float…
The rain I see and the wind

Laughs back sweetness.

That thunder that roars
Above my roof snoops for nothing
But affection
From that green ripe fruit.

Evergreen ripe song
Affection and satisfaction from the lands'
Green ripe fruit
And the green creeping morning breeze
And those silvery dews
Sliding down those
Green leaves
I love.

They are crying. In tears of joy
We all cry
For her evergreen smile…
That green ripe fruit
From the slopes
In the sun-down coast
Where the fields are green
And the birds are singing in the air
For joy is shining
As I sit and sing to the seasons
My emotions
Rekindles the springs of my soul

That evergreen smile:
Pure, humble and chaste…
Come my way, my poem.

Korora

Long
Green. Yellow
Thin without flesh
Basks on mama's trails
On a bright sunny day
To scare ma's spirit away…
This is attempted murder, fork tongue
Serpent. And this ain't your track
Parasite

The Road to Deumori

False fear pangs
That sweat that runs wild
To die in this wind of September days
As you climb and rest your heart
Up this zigzagging ruggedness
To the grace of those singing birds
O my angel eyes
This rains that cleanses
Your loins and the palms that married
Your crying knee
Come from those Ioro hills
Lining the horizon like a march
Of warriors ready to die…
We blame them for sins, they do
So god punish we
With this laughing endless sky water,
My foreign love…
Feign Ioroan.

Calm and pace on
O brilliant song
To those cliff face and orchids and

Crushing steaming waterfalls
And rugged rigid boulders
Of your longest trail
Oh, honey from the east

Just sweat sanity,
O song
Hidden below this smog is joy
That boosts strength for the tribes
To conquer
This Ioroan spine of life
To that desolated sanctum
Of the greenish mountains
And creeping clouds…
My beloved Deumori

Stupid Wind

Hey wind,
The tree dance patterns
O plain mystery …
Bending like lead,
Rolling like a ball,
Jumping like a bounce,
Smashing like a fist
And tearing like a razor
Under my cold nose …
Scattering my dreams
In a gigantic dust storm
As in Sahara storms.

Why this, insane wind?

They spotted you in Africa-
Across the Solomons-
To those Caribeans

Swooping, rollicking, scurrying and frolicking
Every heat beat
In a massive song
That is nothing but wind

Oh stupid wind
Why and why?
I'd keep on crying
As you'd keep on hissing
A serpent song
In the terrible nights
Of clanking confusion to
A morning of cluttering dance
That mama vomits
Her nerves at sighting, oh,
The dirt of your folly…
Stupid wind
Of nowhere but every where

Oh windy, wendy wind
Why…hey, why?
You come rolling across my Bougainville
Laughing insane mad.

Oh stupid….stupid wind!
That stupidity so vast like the universe
Mama, sssh…a clank again on our roof top…
Sssh…sssh…

Goodnight mama

Dongkiringkiring

Dongkiringkiring…
My beloved bird sings
Its name from the highest
Naked branch in the lush
Greenish wilderness
Of Crown Prince Range
O'er and o'er…
At dawn .
Dongkiringkiring…
The echo goes on
Through the deepest valleys
Down my spine
And across my heart…
Dong'kiring'kiring…
That wake call
Before the rooster's welcome…kokore'ko!
Dong'kiring'kiring…
Immobile me in ecstasy
As it fly away
Flap, flip, flop by
Through the air so immaculate
Dong'kiring'kiring…
She knocks on my sad heart
She interrupts my dreams
To welcome the new day
Dongkiringkiring…
She amazingly scratches her beaks
Exquisitely shakes her head
And combs her colourful feathers
Letting go some to the mother earth
From that highest naked branch
Dongkiringkiring…
Her love calls in the wind
Flap and a flip
She flies through the canopies,

O'er the hills
Across the seasons
To the sun

Kosinung

There are times
When I sit and wait
Long hours into the nights
To get a glimpse of shooting stars

In the shrilling miles
Thunder roll and roar and flashes
Like waves at sea

Bats criss-cross the skies above
And fade into the hills
Moving stars-some of them-slowly
Sail and stirrup the heavenly glory
And make me cry

Out of nowhere-
A battle field and corpses-comes my star.
A life…and jets for me

Slowly she warns
Like aging in the flower pots
As she pace lovingly
From star to star giving me new hope;
And life to earth

Tsunami

Floods attacks and kills
Expanse of waste-land scares
Bring eternal grief

Morning Arawa

Look at the gigantic O'voring
That selfish boulder that rises too high
Into the skies of Pava'ire
She smiles greetings to that sun
Glaring behind Po'poko island
That pakia isle

Listen to the si'voi
Singing on the poweline. The parrot
Of our neighbours. She cries hungrily.
As that sun is warming the western brae
And slowly, like a garden snail
Creeping for us
Through the cerulean air
Under the curse
Of the naked Siro'vii cliff
Oh, parrot no cry

See down stairs
The orchids and crotons
Standing with the weight of dew
They are weaken by the dreams of the night
They are listening to the song
Of the next door girl
Splashing away cold water
On her agile chocolate skin

In the kavoro
My talkative sister, Tang'tenani,
Sings hymns to God; her Sunday routine
As she feeds those noisy and lazy sows
Who sleep like me
And never saw the garden

Down on the sun burned street
I can see a man, strolling
For the church in fine fashion
Lonely like a ship
On a widest bay
What good will God gives him?

Life has dawn
Dawn in my town, Arawa
On a brilliant November's Sunday
The sivoi sings
The biring sings, and
The green plants are swaying
Like Solomon dancers

Sun

High and burning all
Midday laughing sweeps me out
Those eyes bring me life

The Unpredictable

"Sun,
the clouds
and the rain
with the blustering wind

is having a feast somewhere,"
mama said to grandma
whilst running away
from that
storm.

Flood Water

Subbing old orchids
Heron's hunger strike season
She pots no mercy

Lake Momau

Amble the groyne
See me by the lilies
So elegant this June
The boulders and mosquitoes, there
So prone to guffaw
It seems the frogs, herons
And the straying, scavenging and mating
Wild family of crocs
Watch those white breasted tavi'tau
Flying higher and higher
In fear of your infiltration.
Renew that nexus
Nestled upon by that wind
To this gift
We call, Momau,
O beautiful children.

Poems on the Bougainville
CRISIS

The Ballad of Bougainville Soldiering

The trigger man. The trigger man. The invading trigger man!
He disembarks tough and fierce…
The OC barks orders
He knows, it's time for the jungles

Those shrubs brushes his face welcome
He sets booby traps and roadblocks
Along suitable garden paths
And waits stealth and eager
For the blood of a black man

For days and seasons he raids…
Eyes directed and re-directed,
By the point of the barrel…
For who there? The Kawas!
As gunships hover high up, and about-
Mortar celling, rumbling ahead and beside…camouflaged,
He crawls all his ways through
Sludge and thorns

Tired of cruel nights, mosquito shrill sickening-
Ambushing nothing but wild bite:
Barking and squealing-- he
Rampages the village innocence.
Burning to ashes magnificent beds…
Gunning down and bye,
Good looking broad faces.
And raping my womenfolk for him fruitlessness…
Flagging the Sepik Tambaran Haus.

A week in the wildest fields
Crying-- tails between his legs-vexed…
But a day off,
He marches intact up and down

The street of my towns and life.
O dastard!

A gun in his right torture and a woman
To his left.
He chats to the penniless blackman: Kawas, you
Trouble men.

Leaving her at morn…
He, to the jungled ridge.

You know brother,
Prolong bombing and blooding bullets,
He cries…
Blast in the tangle
Pins him to the ground
He cries and cries. He cries for ma in New Guinea

Who say she hears?
Poor dog!

Sandline Mecenaries

Island in the south seas…
Brokenville lies here,
In this lake of chaos
Longing for missionary legends
And their kind of god.
Not your lethal warheads
Of mass murder and looting.
Nor that torturing policing rod
As she no feeder of gluttons
Like your darling red sun
Of that killer west…
Oh, you money face killer
She cries for her freedom from redskin subjugation

Of this black inspiration
Dimmed to thinness of emptiness.
She'd struggled
At door ajar, oh, money maniac…
Keep my Bougainville for missionaries…
Not mercenaries'
Greed.

Hideout

Hideout.
In the hideout,
the papa and the mama and the sick pikinini.
save the flowers:
the mister bougainvillea, the black roses
and orchids
of brilliant colours.
O plumage of your dreams
and blood streams.
The future clouds of rain
making to this barren land.
caressed by greed
of intruding savage storms
In repeated fire flight
of uneased raging fist and windy bushfires.
O infernos of uneasiness…
Mastering the rains, nights o floods.
Don ever snore nor scoff
but track on and on
like hunter dogs you'd dreamt of
sniffing in thought
and peeing round
for cool heartedness.
Your roaming sacrifice,
dearest papa creature.

Hideout.
The papa and the mama
and the trembling pikinini…
hear the barks, oh!
echoing through tranquillity,
those are smashing, rocking and tearing
bangs…the bangs of death.
The wildest wails and trickle
of folk blood and tears.
O fallen sons…
smashed and lifted
higher and away'd
like log scraps by grenade.
Dear papa-mama, see
dear torn flesh; God's divine design,
maimed and wasted by bullets…not your era,
bows and arrows
but bullets from Australia,
that digger master of the planet
who want the land hard dwelling.
E, fade of flowers
in the glaring patches
of millions, you'd never saw
you'd born into right
those vivid colours of joy
dreamt of far beyond those horizons.

Hideout.
The papa and the mama
And the weeping pikinini…
keep calm like the coffin
of the frightful odours
raving evil lour
you hear across nights
are the gunships rotoring
and gunboats steaming
through no-man's places

with chronic fungus musket…
to kill they came…o
precisely harm
he forgot the cry of reflex
and sail the farthest seasons
south to snowy heavens
of his masters…
te, digger, whitefella fella
who'd one second twice born
rage and erosion.
In paradise,
those your foe hunters
on the landscape of your living.
Living all days…
to torture and arson and looting
those life giving remnants
and sail away
to kiss his grubby wife'e in New Guinea.

Hideout.
The papa and the mama
and the hungry pikinini…
smelling gaining nothing.
Your patches smoking weep in the green house
made sick ache over and over.
Below …
and backed
by guns blowing racking,
he'd spew off clouds
through streets of curiosity.
Fever fevering,
to hear this red glutton
of the sunset distances.
O infidel saint of the night ways.
He dives and roams in repeated flocking
of yours, house of love
being torched

by god in capitalist dreams.
So hideout,
The papa and the mama
and the dying pikinini.

Island of Tears

Blackman,
A thief in his Africa;
A disease in his Australia;
An on-looker of his pride and wealth on Bougainville
He is…since
Many years ago
And gone…JOY of the LAND.
His progenitors roamed trouble free
From cave to cave;
Jungle to Jungle
With the law of the land
Prevalent in the laughing hearts and
Smiling across all seasons…
This'd very hearts
Of honesty and respect
Now in the boiling pot
Of white man's civilization—free will and free choice—
Of living and dying in peace of relegation.
He gives and teaches
Flowers of expression
Not that black, but white.
Yet, o lord of cemeteries,
An expression,
A sorrowful black man gestures
To earn a wage of living behind bars of blockade;
Hearts pounding o'er and o'er again
Tearful in disgrace,
From ages of mimicry;
Earning a waving legacy

To live and mess in exile.
He dies an animal death
By a legal gunman
Empowered in bulk shipment
Of ideal law
From the perfect God of Zion
That swallows gasping belly
To enrich this hand cups
To sting you generation
Chained in a line of slaves
Dwelling in worst misery hideouts
And filthy slums
Of emptiness and pain …
On the outskirts of your birth right
There you fight and kill
Squeezing your heart
To a strand of extinction …
Sun after sun
Tears storm your beds
Moaning the lost brothers
In the jungle of chaos,
Those petals of your joy
Carcassed by white divinity
Of peace and freedom …
Yet so colourful, Bougainville
Loved it then earned a living
In the harsh ridges…
Hearts sailing
For tomorrow is opaque
Like a fierce storm
Of destruction.

Blockade

That curtain in the land, sea and air
Suffocates innocence in caves
See it infiltration
Fence

Fear Path

Hide the moon o'er mama
And let magnesium lit the nights
Stone all flapping wings
And helicopters soar the skies
Seal tectonic fury
And bombs quake your pride

Oii mama what type ,new type living
In no love like peace
But graves called caves

Oii mama the guard of the land
We'd weeping in the curse of yes-a-day
That colours our Solomon
The land of fear and blood

Oii mama

We weeping
As tomorrow is always doubt
Peace and freedom is blur
And trails pour misery
From those Solomon clouds

Oii mama, is it this?
Longing for secular harmony

O,er the ages of devotion fruits
Peaks of wonderment
As we tangle in dull clouds
And plains of blood bath

Oii mama…
O my Solomon island of Bougainville
O my Solomon island of Guadalcanal
Maimed
Teared
By foreign arrows
Who rave their ways in this paradise

Oii mama,

Why this?
You'd say: "God knows how'd."
But this chokes me, ma'am…
Down through my dreams
Look, children of heirship
Tither to the empathy tomorrow
Of that past greed…
Casted by gone pride horizons?
Oii mama,
look them
Knew'd injustice before harmony
For they nurtured in hopelessness
Dining I the plate of relegation
And lethal guns
That said lamp of hope and freedom
What you say, ma?

Oii mama

You see them kill or killed
For the recovery of that lost pride
No cry , mama

But paddle that boat
Of your deeds

Blackman Street

O blackman
You'd fought and a victor
You'd frozen under jungles of misery
For this women and crates
You'd warrior on and on
Like angry alligators
Needing kneading
From a black woman and riches of the schooners

O blackmen-women
Fumes and screams
Naked and bruised
Blood and tears
Live like you like

O black-men
For I'd live like you
Under clouds of laceration
Oh, tomorrow brings what, mama?
Upon this and that
Lachrymose
Child
I sat down hearted
Weeping
Bemoaning
In the same stinking
Valley of tears
Over and over again
As lowman
Pigsty model man

O black-man
I'd frozen like you did so
In those precious jungles under the rain of gunships
Where blackman cried
Here and there as
Sharpest roots burn our soles
To pain

O black-man
I prayed for o'er the flight of years
In those darkest ridges
Running wild for our freedom
The barrel speaking our verses
With repeated pureness
From high in the ranges
And lower in the shorelines
The streets became black
Blackmen-women

O blackmen-women
The streets of ours with
Smoke and screams
Naked and bruised
Blood and tears
Live like you like
O blackmen
Bleeding out and beyond
My perfect innocence
Spying for no traitors
Just to fetch my woman
And cleanse your jungle suffering
With me a nothing
But a dirt in the screen

O blackman
Driving virgin cabs
Under the nose of our women

You are a fighter…
Snoring in a newest life style
You are a leader
On the heap of war gains
O blackman
Live like you like
For the barrel utters your words
Like before and now
O blackman-woman
Smoke and screams
Naked and bruised
Blood and tears
That colours that freedom screen
For the blackman
O Blackman.

Innocent Still

The New Guinean barrel faces me
And my mouth waters.
The soldier teases me
And my ears burn…
But I am still innocent
Innocent as Jesus.

The New Guinean baton skins my head
And it bleeds furiously.
The policeman chains me up
And my wrist aches
But I am still innocent
Innocent as Jesus

The New Guinean law stool flattens me bums
And it loses me blood o'er.
The law man want me answers,
Yet I know no such crime

For I am still innocent. Innocent,
More than Jesus!

Crisis

Walking this planet, and
Unzipping her hidden follies
I learn that nothing is worse than the bitter
Bougainville unrest
For it ate my beloved
Papa.

Rebel

Cyclone liberation
Casting millions relegation
O brilliant morn
Freedom fighter

Ballad Of Hiding

Run. Run, o run
My children and friends. Wives and leaders

Run. O run
For this ain't your joyful night
But a night of the tearing foe
Who barb your sea and sky
And leach your rights as the sun revolves

Run. Run o run
My children and friends. Wives and leaders
Run. O run

For this ain't your song night
But the hour of rampaging infiltrators
Who pile guns and bullets at your shores
To smear blood on your life
And endanger you species of the land

Run. Run o run
My children and friends. Wives and leaders

Run. O run
For your life is wanted sailing
But those infidel camouflaged eyes
Searching, burning and looting
Your colours down
For him selfish luck implementation

Run. Run o run
My children and friends. Wives and leaders

Run. O run
For this ain't your feasting day
But day of the marara invaders
Who air justice and peace booby traps
And sing songs of love to behead
And blow horn of civilization to rob

Run. Run, o run
My children and friends. Wives and leaders

Run. O run

Care Centre

The rice-tinned fish farm
Growing bulk and sleepy
Beside the roaring guns
Camping

Blood Generation

My child
This my child
Knows nothing like perfect good
But worst
I'd done him be gutpela fellow
But dear god
At the strange wrong hour
Inside the darkest hell
As guns blasted
Deafening him
Flowering wisdom

My child
My beloved pikinini
Dearest god
Knows nothing but cruelty
A smack,
O lord for your case,
He'd return with a knife
Death art stuff, king of peace
Retaliation, you see
O god
No, please

When I say: you sick?
He'd say: the bush medicine

Not civilization at all
Awful!
O lord, what now?
When I say: go schooling
He'd fear the army in town
Oh no!
God, where is you?

My child
This'd my love fruition
But knows nothing divine
But trouble

I sit on my lap
And say: tell pa a story
But horror dawns: uncle was shot death

My love bought him a doll
But he rolled under a cloud of dust
Crying for a M16
He saw him uncle carrying
Dear god
What this?

Yet this'd my child
My pikinini…
Why me and love have
Such nightmare in paradise?

Lord I search my mind
For solutions
But it's you
Dear god
You are the way… but
Ain't you a liar?

But god

It's frustrating for me and love
You say the way is you…
So come with your bushknife
And take this child
Away to paradise
To trouble you there

1989

Widest flooding plains
Rotoring and blast feeding tremble
Jungle breeze drags me on

Peace Prayer

I am longing for peace
And freedom
In my land and life
Of painful injustice
Peace and freedom
In the Solomons and the world

Peace and freedom
Ours and your topic of gossip
Day and night around the world
Peace and freedom
In the Middle East
The land of terror

Peace and freedom
We pray over and over, for
Nothing but peace and freedom

Peace and freedom
In weeping Africa and Asia and the

Land of masters
Peace and freedom
Peace and freedom
My padre talks them
Peace and freedom…but
Driving pass me-
On the streets of strife-
Never stretches him clean palm
For me to beg on

Peace and freedom
In the wireless planet
Mister politician defines in good art
For the crying peoples
But where wind of change?

Peace and freedom
We cry: "Peace and freedom."
But where gestures of peace and freedom
Amongst you people?

Gun on him lap
Terrorist say: "We for peace and freedom."
European say: "I fight for perfect peace and freedom."
Peoples at loggerheads…
Whitepela say: "You terror it!"
Blackpela scream: "We for peace and freedom!"
Peace and freedom, we cry…

Peace and freedom
Clash of civilizations for peace and freedom
Blood and tears for peace and freedom

In the world of hatred and guns
I cry peace and freedom

Let's cry

Peace and freedom
In my land and life…
The Solomons and the world
Peace and freedom.
Come, oh dove of
Peace and Freedom

Poems on LOVE
&
LIFE

Medicine

Purest water
Emergence of refreshment
Prolongs my breathing

Beside Agony

Sweat trickling rolling down
Engines crackling clouding round
As fumes choke life leisurely along

My eyes eagerly penetrates corners
As my soul strolls steadily
Along poverty and pride pavements
Girded by playboys.

Little from simple living and labouring
Chinking in my purse pocket
Just for needs on sojourn
In this world of classes
Of pridemen ruling poormen,
I strive between neither yokes.

At one hundred kilometres an hour
On the busy street-the modern lamp of people-
Jets in tie and white socks
To those signature offices of rob
That changes the world over...

For'd governors and nations…
The bully wives and children
With rotting raging teeth
Along those immaculate paths of high living
Hosting gesturing beggars living on alms.

My soul drifts, on

Nod hunts for left over's
In the bins of tie-men
Relaxing safe from cold
That kills the street's god's creature.

Fronting luxury,
Screen of square eyes
He sits gazing stock markets.

Too many minds of money
He sweats through the nights…

Messaging are the bulky wives
For life going-on kneading, boy.
As simple men
No chronic ailment striking
Travels on as life dictates.

We travel beyond
Beside scare goats
Wet, coughing and weeping and dying-
Breathing just smile-of
Hostile nature gluttons
On the street of civilized fist and rods.

Sitting on never defeated peaks
Across sparkling oceans
He sings
By the heaven of brothels and taverns
That white socks man dreams.

My soul zooms in and out
Weeping to get her fragile destiny
By parks and lakes-isolation and no jokes-
Like country culture.

No hope though,

In serious shocking scenes
Even the rich aches and fades
From beggars begging on…
Looking hopelessly cold.

Of this pure inharmony, e'er, reaped
Bred of modern men for'd him all.
"Oh, stray dogs," I'd told myself.
Feeling stupid
I plop a coin on him scurvy palm
Under the storm of mimicry
And stagger away
To avoid him poor teary gazes
That tears my greedy heart on and on

My soul bemoans…
For the always suffering along,
Those victims of civilization
Casting votes of power
To the evil doer

I'd waded beyond
Through the waters of injustice
To the banks for breath
And restart my eroded ego.

I sit and stare silently
Into the twinkling night hours
That never labour
But happily nourished.

About all peaceful nights
No chinking in my purse pocket
I prone and wonder in tears
About the meaning of life.

Weeping, shivering and gasping

Along the misery of the dark ages
Born by money and prestige
I lamented to my grieving grounded heart,
That life not worth living
For my life.

Daydreams

Silly clouds
Save them for the rainy days
Watch them blossoming
Silly thoughts

Harlot

Little beauty nursed
No chinking; back streeting,
Coffin of bravado

Domicile

A love for a house;
In intense fondness of her,
I run for her.
In fear,
For shelter and
In greed.
But why?
Why not to the charnel house?

Anger

Beautiful bird
I hear stings my heart all night
Those wondersome beaks

Miss Darenai Love

Bompo'rikonang, da bompo'rikonang.
O angel of Darenai

You'd cherished my dream
that long and narrow lane
with no clouds nor rain
to feed my loins
and make new hopes…
carpenter fresh for Poaru'nau.

O bompo'rikonang…my
dream come true…Essam dear.

From the sweetest distant Darenai
you wrote to Poaru'nau-dark in folly-
beautiful inspiring poetry
that portrait deep deep
and flitting love.

These kept me safe
through those long desperate nights.

O bompo'rikonang, sweetest lips and ode
from Darenai.

But why that gloomy April night,
you'd kissed me no more?
Did those Sunday floods and rain
fetched you to Barako?
You smeared me,
that distant love to tears…

Oh bompo'rikonang…my dream…
my shattered dream?

I sat-sometimes-and swept your poems…
once you sent me to Bapong,
those terrible peaks and cold I hate…
Why that, my Essam?

Oh, bompo'rikonang…bompo'rikonang…
heaven at Darenai.

You-in folly-forgot those finest
arts of Tumpusiong poetry.
Those nights of love making and kissing
by the warmth of Tongare
and hark to the dirt of Kavarong,
my faded love.

Oh bompo'rikonang…
You flower in the bareness of bluish Kavarong-
my Darenai love-
Memory will not let go.

Accident

Bougainvillea
Her rest underneath, kills joy
Long isolation

Mi Krai

Papa krosim mi
Na mama rausim mi
Long nambis mi sindaun sore istap
Naispela win i blow
Ol pisin I singsing
Taim solwara I pairap
Tasol bel bilong mi i hevi…I hevi tru.

Long nait mi pilim kol
Insait tumas long bun
Strongpela rain i wasim mi olgeta
Mi krai, krai tasol
Long husat?Mi noken save
Mama i dai na papa,tu
Ol bilak bokis antap
Smel bilong ol olsem pispis
I sore long mi krai
Na mi krai tu
Mipela olgeta i krai
Ai wara ran olsem bikpela wara Kavarong
Na mi go iet . Go we?
Mi noken tok…

Antap long blupela maunten, Oparoma
Mi sanap
Olsem wanpela diwai kokonas i nogat lip
Mi hangere
Na liklik bel bilong mi,turangu i pairap
Win i slip sore
Solwara Solomon i koros
Mama i aipas
Papa, bel i solap na i aipas

Olsem na mi laik i dai
Dai long switpela han bilong win
Em tudak bilong mama
Na bikbel papa

Blinded By Heaven

Padre,
God man.
Snore in luxury.
I travel the planet
looking for life.
As you
dream.

Your love

Girl,
I see us floating away.
Wind blow us flowers.
Round our kissing
You cry
Love

The Magic Of Kunu'nava

Nem'makaa…
the magic little boy
loves blowing his kovi
high in the black hills.
Lusts listening erect
those sinking, rocking sacred echo go
rolling
bumping
crushing pellucid quake!
through the deepest valleys to the kunu'nava
that legend house heat
of mystic chastity.

Scaring away the owl spells
like clouds fading dying
due no adoration dogma
but just chatting
laughing away'd his trespasses.

O magic.
The magic…the magic little boy
who blows across ranges
tunes of strangeness…
anew
mysterious
tempos that retrieve
the blood of virgos;
o chaste magic little girls
from the initiation of kunu'nava.

Amazed.
Shocked in disbelief
and inclined to the verses
of joy sweating; burning and glowing they sing:
o magic…
the magic little boy
come…o'come…
come you magician
of a hundred rivers and slopes.
Come kiss this cone
sharp breast and
caress them to fire
and fetch your share of dreams
and power.

Come… o'come…
come disqualify my holiness.
Smear my lips
with that spell of mystic oils-
the surge of your pride-

that pride…o…pride.

O magic…
magic …the magic little boy.
Come…o'ii bakaa nemakaa,
the heir of my menstruation genesis…
oh boy, o.
Boy of my happiness and heritage.
Come!
O come…by
the taboos of your forefathers
pay your homage
to the night owners-
o killer of souls-
who keep the door of the kunu'nava
as owls of death.

Death. O death…
In the dark canopies, it's death.

Death it is, my magician
Of a hundred rivers and slopes.
O magician,
homage the spells over and over
with the magic flutes
from the blackest hills and peaks of fog.

To the verses, o owl spells,
care for my womanhood,I am the boy…
She owes me the powers.
Pleasures.
Joyful dances
and wisdom potions of rain making –
seasons and life-and prolonged love making nights.

Secure my life,
my good servants of the kunu'nava,

she's the cuddle of my loins…
fattened by the first produce
of the land and seasons.

She is the pride of me , the foreigner.
O magician of a hundred rivers and slopes.

She was, o god
hidden from the eyes of moons and suns…
those broth spillagers.

O, owls
In the canopies of death
Caress my spirit amidst those virgins
Initiating to the mysteries
Of womanhood and
Child bearing pains
After naked sleeping of joy.

O owl spells,
Spirited clouds and fireflies,
Care for my joy in the kunu'nava.
The artery of my testimony.

O magic,
The magic little boy
Of a hundred rivers and slopes.

The magic,
The magic little boy…
He blows
The melodies of dance
To the nights and spirits til dawn.
Sweating erotic hearting
And lust pains blowing to the great land-
Peoples of experience- of women

And smeared thighs,
You'd had it all before the kunu'nava.

The bright sun is over the sea
Coming to rage my heart,
Dry to emptiness.
My tender of dreams
And moisture of pride,
The magic little boy
Company the magic,
To the house of kunu'nava.
Have me sink and lost
Between the lost thighs
And bring forth womanhood of big buttocks.

O womenfolk,
Of skill and endurance
Bring
To the fall of spirited nights
O'er the majestic kunu'nava
And her fountain of life…
That erotic life so long.

Dance in joyful moaning…
O magic, the magic little boy…
Shout and scream and roll…
And cry:
O mother earth
Dance with me to the gate
Of magic and wonders of miracles and gods.
Mother,
Mother earth
Dance with me to the gate of magic and wonders
Of miracles and gods.
Mother
Mother earth
Blow your flute to the kunu'nava

Sleeping like skull
Under the azure sky.

Burn…crackling
Must be your superstitious torches
Quaking beds
To warm the fingers of power
To caress those cone breasts and sweet lips.

O mother earth!
The magic,
The magic little boy
He dances and dances for the gods and spirits
Under the magic of kunu'nava.

Striver

Storming wind
After writing-reading the widest universe
Beyond grasp of those empty drums
Rollicking and pealing my church,
You come…
But why me sweating in stain rags?
As these village colleens stroll in gleeful sunshine,
I sit and sleep…snoring
Wonder in defeat.

Knock On

No girl. No cry
My air is pure blue
My room shines peacefully over all
This humble rain waters all: harlots
And lesbians,
Lunatics and zealots, alike,

Bulky prate politicians and nuns…
So, no girl no cry.

No child no cry
Your falling abode is his curse
To admire my violet wine is divinity
To your sparkling innocence,
My child.
I am the fountain of fragrance.
In the green fields
I am.
So, no child no cry.
No love no cry…
I am calling in the wind
For you to come
And rest on the bed of roses
To laugh and dance
To the perpetual harmony of the jungles
And birds
So, no love, no cry

Arawa

The old dying queen
Toasted sick by stormy seas
Of just mosquitoes, no pity
To my town

One In A Million

The flowers
Those scentious ornaments
Colours my dreams
All night.
When I sit or fly

As the birds do
Across the oceans
To touch a million
Greedily
Like a hungry dog,
It aches me
Deeper,
So when I came home
It was the same
Gleeful faces
Inviting me
From this black hillock
And beautiful
Valleys…
The one is
Better.

Lost in A Million

Proning on a desolated plywood
Palms gripping on to the distant fringes
In the shattered gauntic Arawa bay;
My covetous soul chased
The angelic form of waves
By the sea of frolicking
Gazes of white hungry seagulls.
Those beautiful waves in communion
Sprightly delta my selfish slide.
One love jerks me on
To one meteor of perfection
That widens my frisks on…
For one kisses that black mountain
Of roses in multitudes hastily
And sets unwanted goodbye.
Like that toddler of this naked lawns,
Decanted of promises by Kupe roads

In swooping blustering songs
Of cruel December nights…I
Greedily bark for that bed
Where those brightest petals
Were nurtured …My
Longing eyes swept the rugged
Pidia point about to lip
That servile Dapitotopu as swiftly.
My heart, pounds menacingly
To that gauzy apparition
Of the largest bulge, I touched…
It crushed and faded
Before my perilous surfing.
In complete disarray…
Appears another smile in perpetual mockery
Of my routed folly…That's just
A million roses
Worth eyeing and not
Touching, for it thorns.

Hardly-Lyn and The Wonder Boy

My brother never hide
the reasons in his sane mind.

So, one fine day
By the dragging breeze
Of the mighty Buka passage
He told her pa:
"this wander-boy marry your Hardly-Lyn."

The pa just smiled
Like a bright lamp in the dark
Making the wander-boy
Jump for the moon

The wander-boy never knew she knew
Til that cloudy government day
They met at a distance. Eyes hooked,
By the muddy lawns of Hahela
And Hardly-Lyn paced away…
A lazy heron of the Boi'ra swamps
In gleeful smile of her escorts

Wander-boy nevertheless was in the clouds
"Dear brother, o politician
Is this sowing right?
Is it love
Or simple hate in a fond heart?"

The Wander-boy, though, clouded
Sauntered on.

Birthday

Charming and spurring
The deference blowing life a re-start
I got none
Born day

A Call In The Dark

Girl
My love
Burn all around
You know that well.
Why can't you reach out
And touch that song?
I am calling
In vain
girl.

Baby

Cuddling you is joy
Eyeing the future breaks my heart
Be a sweet child of mind
Love

Jacky

Singing waterfall
I hear takes my heart away
Those romantic days

Bompo'rikonang

Tumpusiong was the pool
coolly pool of gleeful stones
of that smiling affectionate Kavarong river

and Bompo'rikonang was the butterfly, whom
they say-people said-
in intense love of the poem
the poem called, Poaru'nau…
spend twenty-four hours a day and,
seven days in the longest weak week
with the poem…
Chatting and eyeing…
never touching, but dancing…
dancing afire!

By those sweet spells of Poaru'nau…
chatting and eyeing
never touching, but dancing…
dancing afire!
Bompo'rikonang dreamed
of the Kavarong's frolicking poem

in purest harmony
into the coldest nights
gobbling, singing and laughing
for no one, but that Basi'kanung
of the gracious Ioroan valley…
Dancing…dancing afire!

Under mama.
Mama bright…moon ma'am.
Snoring…but sane.
Never touching, but dancing
Dancing afire…
Poaru'nau snored
like oldest ma'am of Kavaronau
scaring away the birds and owls
that rave their ways by the shadow of the poetry.

Into the morn of the brightest sun
chatting and eyeing
never touching but dancing…
Dancing afire!
O'er Ioro ridges-they say-
those ridges of flowers
mumbles those prayers
that are nothing but Poaru'nau.
Smiling by the Kieta's
thousand poets
so far…far away'd.

And slips
like an elver
into the Kavarong dream…
Chatting and eyeing…
Never touching but dancing…
Dancing afire!
He wades between the rocks
and water bubbles.

Against the strongest currents
he swims through the seasons
to the Kavaronau eldorado…

So can you catch him?
I wonder and wonder.

Love At Teng'kona

At ease my mind
one night on the stony
river bank of Kavarong,
I came to face
a girl of the bara'paang clan…
so unlike Ioro lovers-
rosy, energetic and alert to the core-
that loiter in numbers so few.
Angelic was she…
solidly tact and cute…
One of the Ioroan girls
Kavaronau says, fate as ignored
for fast extinction. At her ribs
paced I; taciturn, but
not beyond the gold reefs…
But dull from the days
sweating, cutting and burning.
Intent lover was I…
Mending all ears and walking high
but not that high to reveal my love.
She was lost,
but a memorized oracle…
If not my debonairic loins
deflowering the chastity song
valley should have birthed a tittle-tattle
round our intercourse…Did my
frantic blast of emotions shattered

my sanity of a Ioro-man
and our stately communion of harkbarks,
I should have felt unworthy
playing franks with her
beside those love songs.
But I kept touching that suppleness
to the will of the twinkling stars
that graceful night
as she puffed to rescue
that diversion of uxoriousity
amongst the curious neighbours…
She was curtsy but sly;
but raked my gusto away'd,
slowly but thoroughly
like the fading of seasons….
Till we left heart-in-heart, alarmed
by the distant burning torch;
along our routed follies.
Cracking were my veins…
desperate was my heart for the answers:
Will this guppy be mind?
I wondered if she be forever
this debutante and heal
this crux in this
fragile heart.
(based on *Bull and Egret* by Chinua Achebe)

I'pikei

Coy brae
Mako'osi beseeching your devotion
Opulent comrade
Girl

Orphan

Murky torrential rivers
Wandering by; no beds,
Those hopeless tears

Lost

Desolated isle
I see gives my heart sorrow
That magnificence

Why?

This morning cold jacket
Sat silently looking at the sun
Higher smiling over the peaks
After dreams of the far.
Sat still listen gossip in cookhouse
Of all-in-all garden pride tinkling
From those hated dirt ages sweating.
In that distant hamlet life smoke
Papa chopping pieces
As pikinini piling safe in fireplace
Crackling warmth to desperado hearts
O loving cookhouse salvation!
Sat anew life darkling butterfly
As mama caresses holy rosary
Knocking gods," thankyou"

A thousand times…
Beyond oceans of choice. Praying
Sat calm; odorous peaceful swaying
Counting trails of Calvary stations
For the cold sun shining
Tearing the black suppleness

Of mine coffin some days somewhere.
Sat still and still clouded sick
Wondering some more blister weep
By the rage handles
In the garden dancing life chew-gums.
Sat searching my brains… burning
Lovely birds singing no sweating
Fluttering round this coconut swaying
Peaceful than this sacrificing being
Of me thinking off my conscience
Straining o'er that yesterday gobble.
Sat in air of wonder so deep
Wondering why, sun heat me worn
To poor thin…shrinking slim
Long painful olding hours
Alas!
I sank to ocean snore.

Slow The Days

Speedily brightest days come and go
Sickenly I see them go
For I am afraid to go
Into strangest heaven

Rescue

Navigating eye
Bestow upon me colours
Flabbergasted one

Dirty Love

Time and again
You stand at the pinnacle
A white egret by the sable mire
What do you want, girl?

By the roads where toads rot
Dirty rain wets you all over
So smile at me
Never in a month of Sundays
O liar and a cheat

You came to me like an angel
From time to time, you told me-
In tears-you love me
And that love was burning…
Burning like magnesium
In the murky skies

But then you had me sleeping
A innocent child on your arms
And took my magic away
And sailed across the Solomon sea
Living my heart naked
In a nine- day's wonder

Weeping in this valley of tears…
It appears that true love
Blossoms in the paillasse
Once in the blue moon.

Coconut

Darkest irritating clouds
I see catches my burning throat
Those gloomy faces

Prayer

Precious water
Servile humble servant
The brightest flower

Over Now

Tears rolling
I cried for a night with you
I longed to kiss your sweetest
Lips and hark to rhythmic
Snores by my eager sides…
I travelled all night
Through all seasons
Just to get to you; to
Make love to you…
Isn't that deep deep love doing?
I crushed into brick walls…so
Why and why writing
Love letters?

Want No Woman

Love
And woman…
Will I marry?
Kissing honey and managing fire…
Blurs my mind;
Forget it,
Boy.

Harridan

Red hot chilli peppers
A touch smears my eyes and mind
Those fading colours

Piaru Da Aung

Soul brother
That raucous rugged road to Kupe
Was not of virgin vamps that vanquish
But little left over and not lost
Girley girls of the winds
That blow blurring branding
Dirt deep down your
Dreadful dreamy strolls
Like that of the wandering heron

Ah, soul brother
The rain of this October-
Striking every dawn that falls-
Opens to your dismay. Along
The steps of your hikes, sings
Those odd-looking toads and slithering
Snakes…sssssh…
I hate for blurring boldly my breath
Of longer lasting life.

E, soul brother
Longing for banns
With those uneducated, and uncultured
Bandeaux of those barbaric bally-hoo?
Your lasting love wears lei
And rests in balm
That shall embellish your essence
By the soothing salty springs

Of our violet valley,
Tumpusiong.

Bia Ko Ameai

Rocking minds
All gazes upon your dance
O elated heart
Penny nought!

Slums

Grubby dwellings
Why here, shanty boy?
Heavens gone
Coffin.

The Flower

O hills and brae
Crowned with mist and steaming
For breath of wake,
Decant heaven dull waking
From the long night of dreams
I saw in million times
O'er the Pacific

Lovely is my island of birth
Under the grace of the rising sun
Dancing on air
We the birds
Flapping lengthy wings in salutation
To the blessings

As the land flocks singing high
To quake of liberty morn
Of butterflies and orchids
That scent of deep emotions

Lovely is my island of birth
Cute than honey-mooning song
From O'tong Java atolls
Under the swaying palms.
E, spectacular rolling hills
Flourishing melodic tunes
To canopy giddiness
That dances love
For the stranded

Lovely is my island of birth
Those wild rivers and waterfalls
That born light spectrum
Crushing upon rock mats
In the tropical lamp.
That steaming rainbow poem so vivid
That the saints fall to dreams so strangely

Lovely is my island of birth
Where souls collide in love
By the meadow hang-overs
Of mystic recreation of silver linings
That paints the lovers to lap
Of mysterious dancing babies
I see before dead

Lovely is my island of birth
O heaven of my line
Clouded with paradox myths
For Kawas gist heart
To land of grace;
Wallet of joy,

Willing to seal the sober
To fruition of reason
To the exiled one.

Snoring Love

You snoring, love
I snored too
Looking into the brilliant heavens
Where saints reign
Like biggy bosses
Till that rooster called me: a
Sleeping child under a crystal morning
Kokore'ko!

You snoring, love
In your own perfect world
Your beauty sings innocence
Of tranquillity
Like that of swaying laughing coconut palms
At Tau'sina island
I am longing for…

You snoring like purring, love
Of my lifetime's Darby and Joan deeds
Your waking yawn
Shakes that welkin god
Beyond him conscience

Though still,
You are snoring
My song of calmness
That voice shall borne
The winds and rains that pots fragrance
To my heart's straying emptiness…
O, snoring love.

Rain

Heavenly tears
Clouds weariness wee-wee for weirs
Welcome whipper-snapper
Sky water

Life

Adolescence of rapture
Then cloud of distrust
Why birth of
Striving?

Road Flowers

Bright are scentious flowers
That smile and glee
Like sun on a finest day

As the bee
Buzz by
They giggle and mumble
Their desirous stigmas to the wind that blows
Off and gone
The scent to the clouds of deceitful
Divergence.

Bright are scentious flowers
Petals of, e,
One glance sharp
Picnic…Panicky mooding
Lust glory
Petals of joy
Sepals of vulnerability, o

Look-through
Nakedness
To the retina of the buzzing,
Raging and striking
Electrocuting bee
That are so weak;
Hunger dying
To reap strip the beauty pack
So untouched…
And virgo
For the vaingloryying
Fatherland
Of the sweating patches.

Bright are scentious flowers
Jailed in a patch
To secure lustre
Off birds eye viewing.
They are restless
Hint finding
Like thunder of no storm…
They roar
Quake
From finger tipping
Those conical breasts
To win swarms
That come planting nothing nor weeding
But lucky escaping
Dead strikes

Bright are scentious flowers
That perfume the pubs
Pride of the sailor pa and mama curious
Of her sibling…
Longing for grams of gold
For her bred of petals
Yet no hearing, he gets

From cleverly brats

Bright are scentious flowers
That sway to the breeze of morn
And comb to the moon
Of seasons
Peeping
For never ending hours
With that heart so foreign
Joy killing and
Disastrous

Bright are scentious flowers
With petals of joy
In the gardens and yards
That perfume the streets…
When baby cries…they is go
Skinny sick.

Hutjena

When the sun sets lazily
O'er Solos black ridges for sleep
And the night flooding in peacefully…
That frolicking sea,
Never rests massaging
Those Hanghan women
Behind the very backs of their men

Why is it playing pranks down there?
I felt sorry for them and me
As the chalk never mercy me as them by the sea…
As for them by the sea…the chalk was kneading me,
A straying Kieta boy
All day and into the nights.

Highway

Prone to vomiting
Nauseated, I secretly weep
Since time is breaking its banks
By the road

The Bed

Stuck and locked
In a never ending ravine
Yet surfing o'er waves
Of the blue sparkling Solomon sea
Strip by erotic erosion
And expose to the wacky will
Of my lover's walk-over.
A slice of my brain
Froze to depletion
By her gorgeous kneading
Kindling kicks and knocks
Of consciousness
Til living life alive
Dawns
Like volcanic uproar
At the exquisite swap
Of inner gooey goo
Of baby making messages
O lover
I run my tongue
Upon your naked suppleness
Where desire interprets
As we sail on and far
Let our legs oily in tangle
Lips sticky in kissing
Barter the pillow of romance

Let me suck your saliva of revolving resurrection
What you say?
For I
Am trembling in love
No words to voice,
But love
That soothes
Loneliness
O lover
Sweetest heart
Sing me a song
That shall endear your aging
And have me wrapped
In a cuddle
O angel
Of all clans
Let Makosi not fade
For a second
From those sweetest lips
O lover
Whisper me a poem
To boggy upon your grace lakes
Floating in pure love
Let me drift
Into your sweet world
That is wide
With inspiration
O beautiful woman
We'd jammed in Eden
Across the hillocks of Solomon
Seasons come and fade
For your eyes to discourse
And my eyes to glean
O dear
Keep me warm
With your chest tremours…
My heart is thumping

My love
You water of thirst
To the Solomon fields
Kiss me once and again
So I'd never e'er
Gad about
The expanse of the Solomon sea
My loveliest
Dream.

Death

The thief of the dark
Packs and fades
Speeding days looms me in
To rest

The Cat

Purring fierceness
Barricades the dirty mice
Marvellous staircases

Solomon Dancer

My Solomon dancer
Oily shiny your skin
Cool your lake of wisdom
Pliable your chocolate shape
Cute to floating in bed
To the new tempos.
You are my dance
For the romantic art of caressing

You are the choice
By the smell of siri'vi
You are the song from the myths
My Solomon dancer
Under the mercy of the moon
Sparkling like Kavarong
Your skin.
Shaking your body…
Retunes the world
Rocking your bums…
Sets me sailing
Stumping your feet…
Awakens the spirits.
So let me come
To love and to cherish
My Solomon dancer
Oily shiny your skin
Cool your wisdom
Agile your skin
Cute to the love making nights
Come indulge my rising moon
With the night blend of joy
That surge of pride to me
The beget of your fruit of dance
With a finger on your nipple
That spring of mysteries
My Solomon dancer
Festoon me with the oil of holiness
And let voyeur freedom
To the locale of our dance
But assert my uxorious heart
Forever,
My Solomon dancer.

Farewell Love

When the sun fades
Like steam down Darenai hillocks
Birds settle for spell
Up Tona'ua brook
Those lazy siblings at U'nang they seem

By the dark hours
I sit and watch the silhouette
Features of Darenai hills
Those bats that fly over me
The fire flies that swarm about
Are the hungry piglets at Barai'vaina
But still, it's routine
They say…

They'd never told me
Why I see the horizon
Those sparks of lightening
Mama never explained
My wife never did so
Though her spirit knew
The reasons

Those tales never revealed
The dawn of misery
Til I cuddled my motherless child
Off that tear mat
And ice cold mama
To pacify him.

The sparks of lightening dawned
That my wife was long death
And she was
Idled.

Come My Way

E're, girls of Friday nights
Called : "Friday number nai'nammung."
With penny in my aging pocket
And these boys of drinking sprees
Na dates by the road sides
Cock-aa-du-da-doing
My one second love

I often silently watch you go
Into the icy dew of dawn
Cock-aa-du-da-doing
Your dance babe-one
Second love I tag it-
My the cool morn breeze
Of purling Birimpi brook…

Under the moon; the rain we go
Cock-aa-du-da-doing
My one second love
Before the night is over and pa's
Cock-aa-du-da-doing
Is over in that silhouette
Abode of my birth…

But girl,
You are the pride
Of your ma's
Cock-aa-du-da-doing and life-a
Treasure of your clans' heritage.
Why you dirt your price, cock-aa-du-da-doing?

On the gravel,
The creepers and coldest dew
You are-girl-
Cock-aa-du-da-doing

With those uneducated and penniless
Flocks
Of the distant places…

They flock in-birds of a feather-to
The banks of Birimpi
And drink to the lust
Of your smiles and beg
For liquor…
They is the beggars in Calcutta, girl…

E , girl go on
Cock-aa-du-da-doing
And blow that precious balloon
And I – a civilized boy-
Shall laugh
Til those rocks of responsibility
Come rolling to your mama's
Innocent
Feet.

Wind

Rollicking dances
I wonder where it comes from
Refreshes my breath

My Child

Weaning flowers
Kissing replenishes soul
Those wonderful eyes

Queen Of My Heart

To the girl in Kupe
I authored a ode to you
After crossing the range of adversity
Behind those mountains
You'd mushroomed
For a ink of wisdom
Neglecting the Ioro chest of knowledge
Let go that lies…
And come over grope my heart
You nadir of Kokore
With that smile of love
That stole my hopes away
O colleen on exodus
I wandered in a fragile bark
Over life's tempestuous seas
Til you bloomed bright in bliss
To barb my pace
You the triumph of living
The dance of my spirit
And heaven of my faith
E, fortress of seductive skin and gaze
O nadir in prime of life
Aid the weeping child
Should pleasure's siren hoot
Cuddle the heart of Pomong
Under the sheet of incense
Run your rite
O goddess
Over the bemoaning boy
And purify my blood
O tears of joy
On the bed of your kisses
O nadir of Kokore
Hope to the dreams of Pomong
Finger of sacredness

Tear off my holiness
O nomadic flower
You foreign honey in Kupe
Denude me all
In a odorous storm night
Below the branches of fruition
Our bed of love
Come over grope my heart
You nadir of Kokore
O rain to the heat of Pomong
My black rose.

Cry

God
You see
What I am now
You took me pa away in the wind
And gave me nothing
In return
Zero

Mass

Violet petals
I see enriches my mind
That chilling drama

Wet Blanket

Beautiful waterfall
Perplexes my dream lover
Those harebrained angels

Heaven

O beautiful dance
Raining waterfall of blur
The disturbing hope

Folly Night

That night
Was long and clouding
Like bitter medicine

He said we drink sour water
After our lucky escape
At that old Pi'ne bridge
On the highway to Ioro

He drank and I drank
But I not know he drank
My way before me came
At the singing mountain bar
With me parasite boy
Riding on me back

I realized than they
That the night was clouding
To me belly
And went sleeping
Til morning came

We met
Our eyes met
Him drunk and I sicky
Of vomiting the night
At the swaying fence

And gazes
So sharp to tear
Me down

And she as there
She uncle and she danced
At him abode

Remembering him promise to me
He looked around
To me
Him niece so beautiful
As the rolling hills
Of Kaspeke I admire
Saw not me
But the black clouds
Drifters from nowhere
But slums of inferiority
In Ioro

I see
Made me heart grow weak
And shivering
Like I caught fever

He had me to her
Talking her to me
To make unto her wild love
Though love was burning
I was too sly
Than a rain of shyness
And saved that communion
For the distant
Unknown
Rainy days

Night

E, night
In you is evil
My daughter fears and hides
Til morning

November Eleven

Skeleton Hilux
Stranded people stood amazed
Sang me injury

Pother

Obnoxious chap
Slings poor bat's innocence
Down the hills
They dive; feathers straying
Just like crashing airplane
They go
To his self-delight

He steals green fruit
From ma plot
In those cloudy mountains
As rain falls

He troubles the night… prowling
Raping that harmony
Like mice's misdeeds, over and over
To the warm tears of infants
And mama's nightmare
To the sound of falling ripe fruits

On the iron roof
As she cannot differentiate
The types

Across Bougainville
The evil lizard
Storm the windows and lay
Beside her log daughters

And to the deafening scream
He darts like an arrow
Across the sleeping loams
And snoring bushes
Tails locked behind those evil legs
That highway dust

Forever cold, he is
Under the burning sun
That is nothing but glaring shame

Lullaby

Low tide marching in
Heavy rain clapping in joy
O healing stranger

The Sea Has For Me

Boats cut clear
Crystal water
Foamy soft
Speeding angrily
East
Sometimes calmly west
Other days

Round and twisting and snarling
At the grace
Of the sun and moon

I go rowing
At the will of that salty water
Straining my strength
To the rhythm of my heart

My canoe cuts and ducks
Into the myriad of wavy bulges
So finely greenish
And crushes white
As the Roro'vana sea shore look
From Karo'kataa
Hill road

Hardly my senses note
Those dangers of dreaming
These mysteries of lion sea mood
Yet the further most mystery
Is the brain-wrecking
Brilliant abundance
Of this Pacific ocean.

The Elopist

The girl of my life
The mother of me pikinini
Cuddling
Perfect like the wilderness
Lips crimson
From betel-nut chewing
Coal black like night
Sweet tender character
Mind you…

Take me lewa away'd

Out there alone
On the gravels of Tumpusiong
I sing to you,
Love
Flowing down your spine
Amidst the night of shrills
I sing
To your soul
Come and let we kiss
And run away
Into the twinkling night
Under the gracious moon
Pack, o love…
Get out far

Let your ma snore her rage
To the deserted pillows
As we travel on
To the oasis
To make love
Beside the springing fountains
Of Dora'ro

Set sail
O love
The author of my joy
Away from the grasp of storm
To the orchids of Toro'ba'u
To strip
And kiss as angels stare; Jealous.

Happy Hippy Lass

Happy hippy lass
My sugary lollipop, are your thick lips
My resting pillows, are your cone breasts
My leisure music, is your loudest farting
Oh! Happy hippy lass.

Life

My grandpa
Died many years ago
Along this road to no-where
Life and its secrets

Then went papa
Somewhere by this trail
O'er those same mountains and valleys
Amongst those beautiful hills

What did they fear and leap?
On this track, what?
Those lilies?
Or that crushing wave at the beach?
What are great insanity was that!

But next shall be mama
With silent folly,
Will fear something or a mischief
What then?
Nothing glittering…

Then shall be me or you
From that unknown foolishness
That shall strike.
We all succumb to her…

Life and her mysteries.

Misogynist

Street flowers blossom
Hate blurs that sweet smell of rose
Night wind drags me on

Friday Nights

Listen to the party
The dancing mass
High spirited
Twisting
Kneeling
Bending stylistically
To the echo of rocking songs
Are those big and shaking bums
Of the colourful lilies

See the air they breath
The dancing mass
Lust torching bright
And ground shadows
Caressing
Hugging
And kissing calmly
In the song of liquor
They gobble beyond
To grab the heart
By the blustering banks of kava'rong

Find the trail they'd disappear along
That dancing mass
Heart afire

Nakeding
Lying and rolling
In liquor lies.

My Lost Memory Girl

Mako'osi
Was the beacon in the storm
High in the waves of distress,
Pleading
Fleeing
From flight of curiosity

Boy, o she disoblige
With my warming fires,
As you'd know-
Sweet, tender, gracious and loving-
Like papa's.

E , you girl
From the distant Birosii
You cry
We know the purple peaks weep
O'er your plea as
I was the sole shining snazzy beacon
You had in that heart
Down the mighty
Plains of Nago'bisii.

But girl my song…
I gave wonderful etiquettes
Yet no fresh ethereal
To price your love

In this bright and promising moon
And that distant silence,

When do we kiss?
Love, by January is a shrinkage…
At the O're… is hate nor love, so
Let the dirt in your beauty eyes
Fade…
Plunge
Into plunder
As I no platonic,
Woman.

Song of The Raindrops

Mama,
The raindrops…
See them falling
With speed and anger
From the thick black clouds above
Where birds sing no more…
Grandma burns no more…
And papa sleeps more
Because those stupid leaves
Are moist, but
Smiling away
As the wind blows by…
Mama , why?

An Adroit Candle

Time and again
Sharp words blaspheme grandpa
As a behind the times
Dank!

But I see the storms knew him- an
Adroit candle.

He sleeps with him pipe smoking
As the wind gusts
Our belly of folly
To absolute strife

But he laughs… no
Grandpa, no
Give that necklace and I will sail alone-a pique-
In the fiercing
Aghast storm.

Moon

Cool eyes
Mastering the stars high
To my dismay
Lunar

Stranger At Night

Strange was the air we breath
For our breakfast
Bread and buttered scones.
Mysterious was the blessing breeze
That blew from dead blue
Unsteady was she as seen
By clear distant eyes.

Why was mama perspiring
Over and over again? Why my
Lapun papa sleep-walking our house
Like a immature child?
Their spirits, may be were drunk…
But that screaming?

The cat and the dog
Who regularly scream and fight over space
In the fireplace
Knew something

Those strange sounds and movements
The wild wail of hens
And that dusty dog who springs into the house
For safety and a bark
To scare off fear downstairs
Why?

Who might be this evil?
Or, is my fantasies or thoughts
Of insanity?
Who knows? I know…You know.

On A Date Bed

At menarche,
Down the road to Toku…
On my bare hands
That gloomy day, for god's sake,
I whispered to Essem:
"In love we are…where there's will
There's a way
Along oddities of life.
My girl, no rides as you may think,
On a bed of roses…
It's not a bed of roses I give."

She said:
"We no skylarking. And two heads
Are better than one with mature laying out.
My cup of honey is you. Together, every cloud
We see has a silver lining."

And we kissed on and on…

She was clone a better stock
Of the bompo clan
The sun never disbanded off Tumpusiong
With their inferiority of the land.
As other clans see for joy; I,
For marriage of rearing.

" Essem, as long as the clouds exist
You is mind. The sunshine
Of my morning brace," I said
With my fine works of caressing.

"See my hills and gullies
Of precious stones and spices," I sang unto her,
"are bound for your womb,
My only candle in the dark."

"And so it be, my love."

"Yes, my flower in the sick bed."

I cuddled her into sleep
Of brilliant pages of dreams
To the hopeful
Sunrise.

Bougainvillea

My island memory
In the foreign killing fields
I love you
Flower

Hug

Habitual cry
Guzzles my halcyon gulch
Lover infiltrates

Rabis Meri

Naispela pes
Na tanda I pairap mo
Mekim mi bel krai

Movies

Those talking shadows
Blurs our sunshine season
To the actor's bread and butter
Picture

Trupela Meri

My girl
Say no word in bed
But kisses the clouds out of my bed
Forever

When Will It Dawn?

At Poaru'nau
February nights are often lonely
And long…
Outside the perturbing insect shrill
Truckles to the vigorous and diffusing

Cry of the mining water.
I see no trees that engulf
My home at day light
Nor the fireflies.
But the days are sweet-
Swaying a swing song-
To my broken heart .
But desolated I am
In a deserted domicile of spirits
Waiting for a succubus's
Hour of fun
Near
Mama's breaking
Dawn.

Essem

The high moon
Save my soul, o god
In agony I am
Love

His Perfect World

Leaving that shell of awkwardness,
that long and narrow
road of beautiful colours
that hasten to fade
before the orchestra
of deceitful scorn… he laughs.

He could smile. But too sly
to provoke your power
of pretty pussing
down the road of colours.

Brilliant than the rainbow
O'er Mount Moi'siring you taste…
those night hours; but
the chunk cowardly strolls-sometimes staggering-
for sleeping Onove.

Yet the storms blur
him dream.

A Tale Of A Mako'osi Boy

By the east end
Those mountains and boulders
I see blurs my eyes

My loins moans
To the spirit of the death
New songs
Grants nothing
For the nine-days wonder.

When she sang
A fine weather verse
I cried
In the near distance
I hear peals of thunder
And seek refuge
In the barrenness of her hate
That calmly beheaded the errand boy
To my smile
She cooed through the seasons
Preening those feathers of laughing
Dead or squall.

The Lost Child

Twice gave me hope
Two nights
O fine nights
Striking and penetrating my flesh
Deeper and deeper
My dream come true
Why fade?

Forgive Me

Love
To err is human
and time
pains the true colours; my love,
just love me
until it hurts.

Liar Girl

O liar girl
Snarling and conning
Like February winds sweeping we mad.
You gave fake hopes
By the Tumpusiong roads
So wondrous
In colour and not nature.

O liar girl
Staring is the moon
As you gesture love.
Take me hand to you dance
As your ma burns

In fury
Of your love folly.

O liar girl
The arrow of your sweet words
Hurts me so…that
I bleed in mockery.

O liar girl
Singing to the dance
You sing: "Honialla."
For Honiara…
As you got short tongue
O uncivilized colleen.

O liar girl
Dress like a English model
Yet you no speak foreign talk
Like me do
Nor read between lines
A stanza of poetry I write
O kaulong het
Bush kanakana.

Sex

Night falls to cover
Spirits come to scare and laugh
God you are foolish

Longing

Stain my eyes
To a squint
Of vigorous virtue
To pore over deep into your soul
And read every ripple
Under that robe;
Your loins…
Love

Sales Girl

Sales girl…
O sales girl…
By the counter you smile-
nice row of white teeth,
petitioned by that purple tongue-
so bright and lovely…
I admire you
cos you are a singing sales girl
in a dull town of Ara'ba.
My sales girl…
O sales girl.

Karanas Valley

Every morning when I wake up
I like to go and yawn at the veranda
Of my mountain hut at Doraro
Eyeing the sleepy valley of Kavarong
Down at the hill's foot.
At the glare of the sun,
In the dew filled and chilly east
She blinks…blinks and stretches, far and wide

Then she realizes that I
A cheeky lone boy
Is gazing at her weak movements
With racking interest.

She laughs at me
Over and over again, and
Calls me to a game of peek-a-boo
And like old pals
We sink into a pure orgy
You'd never seen across
Smiling
Joyfully dancing
Karanas valley.

Loneliness

Hunger cramps burning
As evening cries drags me
O mama, come back

Flower

Beacon in the hill
You utter the words I love
Never die young, son

Old Papa

Papa…
Papa, day by day
You shrivel
To wrinkles and wisdom
That shall nourish this land,
And me

When you rest,
Papa.

Moni

Greenish violet lawn,
Fickle the breeze that soothes me…
So when she frays
I go down and down, nah,
To the land
We
Beg-beg

Mother

Mother,
Ain't a whisper in the wind
But a song
Of infinite love and hope.

A flickering candle light
In a dark moment
Is always,
Mama.

Dew

Morning dew
You barb me legs cold
To the creek I shiver my pride
To your caress, o intruder…
But I laugh
As you fade
To the sun.

Poems on Bougainville
POLITICS

The Colour Green

The distant Mai'rua boulder…
That slope behind her;
Are all green

As is my plot of taro
The banana and yams; all
Grow green
And die to talk green
For the dawning progeny

We all sing to green
The old…the youth and the clergy
Love her…but that stranger?
Why is politics turning green?

Anywhere, as the poor weeps
Alongside green,
We all ponder
In purest wonder. But…
Thank you,
My politician.

All The Lies

During the Bougainville conflict
They killed papa and wounded uncle
In the name of freedom

There were many, though, who suffered
And died
And all swept away by the flood

Of time
For good of the of the environment,
The culture and so on and on
As they say

My papa and uncle stories
Are far too many waste of time
The bushes you burn for fun… the
Non-Bougainvillean disco nights
You dearly enjoy, shall not recover
For my crying heart

In the breath of our sea-girted island
We live and die on,
There are too many teary eyes, I see…
For the smoke that blankets
Our hills in the sunny days
And those road side children

In the name of freedom,
Ha rabis freedom; no body nurtured,
You created this mess
In the land of our gutpela progenitors

E, with that freedom
We still cry….

Politics in the Water

This is my journey
You see no rain
You cry
Just like me

No pa in the silent abode
You spill over the lines

And face the music
From your soul
Since morn is clouds scattered
Just like me
Your blood brother

But there is peace always
Amongst the stars
If you miss the moon
This is my journey

Friend and Me

My friend,
When my papa was killed
By the guns in the heartland...
I was a nothing
To the politicians
Absolutely, a wanderer
Of the barrenlands

Under no rain
Of justice, reconciliation and freedom.
I sauntered
To invoke my kind
Of gracious rain
To bath in--my friend--
My own freedom.

The Dora'ro Boy

Gush of winds
worships mi
Over and over again
As you cry in joy

Before your high gods
That sings six feet under your sole
O lone boy in the ridge…you
Nice a bachelor

You know no gossip
Of politics…
Of women…
Of money…
And family affairs,
But your plot of kote'u, koro
And bi'aang are routinely embedded
In your uncombed dreadlocked hair
You nice are bachelor

You want no people talk
And travel the night
To and fro
With bats and fireflies.
You friends in good and bad moments

You fear no dead
And travel your folly
As we stare in wonder

O lone boy,
You nice a bachelor.

The Desk

Funny wooden stuff
Idle and ignorant seat of knowledge
For three hundred or so days
She is mine
Coz mama want me do so
And steal those tressures

She hides for me
O wooden friend
I love you

My Hope Dream

One night as I lay asleep
There dawn to me a dream
That kicked my heart for the moon

In it the world was peaceful
The sea was caring
And air was kind

It appeared there were no cliffs
Storms or disaster
To turn a cold eye on

Beggars and politicians were in
Drop-outs and winners were in
That opportunity bon voyage

I saw that bani'areng'ko-the teacher-
Was not hostile

But one thing mushroomed:
He needed me and I needed him
To conquer the world

So the truth came in:
That I a drop-out boy
Must sweat my guts to embark
The ambition vessel
Sea bounded

In a blinding flash of light

It dawned
That every heart has freedom

Fireplace

Beside sicky ignorant pa
The croc sun worshipper
That burns…
I sit and pen my thoughts.
I sit and pen…
When the world is cold. Gasping.
Dull and cloudy o'er and o'er
In his weaky dimming senses
From freezing cold trails
Lull and gloomy…
Heart faced down
To thought of death….

Oh, but the lunar ball up there
Round and humble
Round and flickering fire
He is a pack and tap of promises
O lukewarm smiling servant
Pulls me, the dirt on
The rim of brilliance

So I write
My dreams and faith
Declining in her
Beside his bundle of pain
O ebbing waters of perfection
My weeping pride
May I compose
The pillars of concreteness?

Where my country folk?

In the expanse of solidarity
And floods of erosion
That pierces my heart to shrink,
I weep her Ways in puzzlement
Stealth and sobering
Deep in the foul cells of disintegration
O adopted grief!
But I swim on.

I sit under the moon, crying
I lament your souls
I sing my loins out
Cherished by the fire embers
You'd call uncivilisation
But sick is that sun you love
You homage her through the nights
As I dream
Your infidel soles tell me off
To stumping dark.

O, you people
People of Bougainville
Weak and deaf
In harmony you are fading
With your croc sun songs
Blinded to death you are
By those fabulous sounds of infidelity

So I pen and pen
From the boiling waters
Of your cruel fate
Those songs you love
Drifting far
The hostile coast and ranges
Of black mockery and muck
You call civilization
Of high hill sophistication,

I call : The harmonious killer!

My people to pride protestation
Strip off that cult coats
In those harsh havocs
And sit by the fireplace
Comb by her wisdom
Flowering under the humble moon
Dip in chest…
Violet words
From long wigged lores

O my people slaves
Drink in the cup of rain
Neglected long
But pouring in bliss
Like waves that gave life on the beaches
O'er and o'er again

Bury the ages of wicked wisdom
O hearts of stone
On the street of sore strife
In love and life of loneliness
That the fireplace knew before you
He is a curious culpritic cold chest
Fake!
Too far from the heavens
Of this'd fireplace.

Freedom

Freedom
That experience
Is a sweet word.
All is looking for everywhere:
In church, in government…
We go
Searching.

Mining

The valley of dust and rock
That makes me ache and cough
Off my pride
Into the pit

Love Freedom

Darkling green brae
Precious, chaste and humble streams
Cockatoos steer my eyes

A Song From Bougainville

My song was sang
In Vanuatu, Fiji and New Caledonia
But loom bright here
This my lyric of pain roses
From deep within my heart cry
Wounded by New Guinea storms

Rising fierce in the western skies
The, sick stench
Crumbling for my house of love
Lone in the south seas

This was my love cry
In the irritating inky ocean
To you revolutionaries
Of my Solomon
With Vanuatu, Fiji and New Caledonia
Folklore nights shivering long hours
O fading flowers in the fallen patches
Moaning in relegation
Are the colourful roses
Suffocated and sick

My song
From deep within my heart
To you freedom seekers
Raging the peace ocean to set
Generation pollens in the azure sky
In grief and doubt
You sing and dance to this lyric
Tempos of newest hopeful smile
Under this glutton sun

This is my song
Song of just salvation
In the new world of my identity
I dance
Dance to restart the birth-dead
To sail beyond the sunset
For purest salvation stored in the hills
But that love for the embers
Sitted release calm
Dancing at knocking love
As your sins away'd

Longing flower sailing
Into this silent love harbours
For honey

This my beloved tunes
Into this sparkling harbor
Lingering heaven beyond words
Calling in the wind:
"Stand up,
O flowers who cry…
Gun the cruel ravaging wind
To her dirty roots.
Dance over the defeat
And sprout from the rot you…good heart
Bright in the dark."

My Panguna

Oh Panguna,
Panguna…
Home sweet home
High in the mist crowned peaks
And black ridges
Girt by seas of dazzlement.
Once a virgin
With your colour green
Of stringent pureness
Robust faith fountain sprinkling
For the proud mama
That erased to nought
The thirst of the land
With welcoming cries, shrills and flappings
Of the wild heavens.

Cry then Panguna
Tears of shivering hopelessness

Slumber e'en in the sludge
Of sorrowful lamentations
For you, my land, life and hope
As been stripped
For the gluttons
To a defiled
Harlot of the streets
O Panguna
Your riches of gold and silver
As ruined us
To the will of foreigners

My Panguna
Of the azure sky
After the rage and struggle
You are sited…
Bums on your rosy remnants
To feed your injured children
In the horizon of the confused aftermath
O sane heart
Together we fight and die
For your liberation

My Panguna
Home sweet home
Of the Ioroan blood
Sing to the hills
Pretty faces and masks
For my girl has returned
From exile
In the land of Paangka
Amongst her kura'baang people
To Panguna
My home sweet home.
Dance.

Asian Liars

I think
You were human
Down history road.
Once colonised and enslaved.
Subjugated you were…
People of the great Asian land
Who bitterly blooded
For freedom.

But why?
You had doctrines, so sound
Invented in the snowfields of Siberia;
Befriended one power in the cold war
Then shut your door kingdom as
"Asia for Asians" and
Fought for freedom?

Hitherto you fought the imperialist man
Screaming wildly
In Israel,
In Afghanistan, and
In the tangle of Vietnam.
You fought and bled for freedom
You said vividly.

But why,
Deserting your birth country,
"Asia for Asians"
Like a insane fellow
And risk your life
Floating across the oceans?
Boat fellow, you
Fear that long sounded

Black Saucepan

Fireplace master
Saucepan. Saucepan; the black saucepan
They called him the darkest monster
Camouflaged unease of the long nights
The cry of terror…
Was the jet-black deeds
"who the god you are, o colonizer,
To see the terrible dark spider
Raving blackness about the night
Beside your snoring?" Saucepan cried.

"Sable saucepan,"
The teacher of civilization
Calls him from morn til noon
With shining teeth and smiles
That tear him deep down those vulnerable heart
In iterated punches.

He the black bastard of this land
Made fool
Relegated to reddish wishes
Jolts the streets in pure disgrace
Pondering his wills
Under the infiltrating sun
Of burning gages and giggles
Of whitefella
And his cheap navies
And slumist of hourly roaming
In this black Eden.

Saucepan.Saucepan, the black saucepan
"Dusky, getting off his old routine,"
They say. Proud hearted in gleeful, cheerful stupidity
He passes to the backseat- where he belong-

For painful driving hours
Amongst padded redskin slumist
Of the dirty outskirts
For the rush hour to Kieta.
That town,
Inky before the plop of modernity
Smeared in dirt sophistication now.

Saucepan, saucepan. The black saucepan
Fireplace master
This is where you belong.

Living On A Prayer

My heart is steadfast; o children,
hark to the song and music
and surf by those gracious waves.

Breath by the new dawn.
Across the sky have eagle pinion
that the Lord whispers to pure souls.
O brother… brother.

The brightness of your orchids
and that sweet smell of sanity
shall conquer the stars
and dance the laziest of stars.

In triumph I will laugh at New Guinea
and slice meekamuism to barrenness;
and let Bougainville free
from dirty oppression.

The Bane'kana fountains are mind…
Beautiful Monahe is my domicile.
Heaven is my sanctuary

and New Guinea, my grubby washbasin.

Come, o steadfast lyric.
Trample down to dirt our foe
as our sceptre
is too fine a phrase:
"living on a prayer."

The Gun

Lethal and black
Hissing on weak arms
Emblem of blood and joy
O musket

Ballad Of Kavarongnau

We pray, weep and sing
To you o Lord
The master of the skies
Enlighten this yoke upon this family
My brother and Bougainville

We pray, weep and sing
Into your deaf rotten ears
Why you gave us this burden
For you to dream?
Poor siblings of Kavaronau
In chaos we cry and cry…

We pray, weep and sing
From depth of broken hearts
For you our blind creator
To enrich the Kavaronau politics
And purify our sturborn hearts, Papa

We pray, weep and sing
At the door of your golden palace
Bring us eternal peace
And guide us on
To oneness of heart
Be our candle in the dark

We pray, weep and sing
To you o Lord of Kavaronau
Amen.

Peace

Longing for hug, sea
At death flower blossoms bliss
The path of freedom

Keke'reu

Guava,
No surprises
Is a mountain frog
King of the dark caves.
Screams melody on lunatics
Killing all
Lamps.

Servitude

Hefty rainfall
Lagoon waves sprouting nightmare
Outside wind singings

No Flower But Guns

O papa,
There is rain in the air
The green loam is smiling, too
But that stranger is weeping
At that pillory

Down hearted
Proscribed and carnaged-flower less-
And pining.

He seems to be a poseur-
O'er the hills they come-
For muskets, papa,
That are nothing…but
Bundle of roses.

Kabui

Darkness candle
Keep me blood running
Light of inspiration
Politician

The Bougainville Game

O Bougainvillean game
You'd kicked,
Knocked and punched
Me off and over
The stool of knowledge
And damned and staggered me
While a little child

For the jungles
Of chronic misery
A sloshed slugged
Breathing
The air of mockery

O Bougainvillean game

You'd tortured, raped and bloodied
My loved ones
Every day and night
Guns,
I hear and cry…
Blood bath, I partake in
Those killings of survival…
Havoc fields
Ambushes and
Sniping and
Beheading cultures

O Bougainvillean game

I see no hand in the shadows
But gun barrel
To spew death
Upon the land of fading oneness
Abode of corpse
Slayings for prestige and heritage

O Bougainvillean game

In the valleys, hills and islands
I hear grief
Of mothers and children
Bemoaning the youth
Fallen in the name of freedom
They cry

Too weak and worn
As more death come in

O Bougainvillean game

Pacifica

Call me, Pacifica
E, ocean of love
Take my hands and knot them
My breast, have them
Your pleasure pillow all seasons
For the world was your god's
And that sun was his lamp
Through the plains

But my dreams,
O lover of highness,
Was planted in the wigs in Vanuatu
Soiled differently in the Fijian dances
But brightly crystallized
To a Bougainvillean heart
Yet quelled in New Caledonia

For this I say,
O evil advocate
Swim the Pacific storms
Blooming everywhere all colours
E, for your romantic verse
So thrilling to seduction
Kisses the foul in the coffin
And repeals
The meaning of love for your case
Through all ages

Though, still

Call me Pacifica, e, ocean of love
With its own flowers of joy
You traitor
O writer of fake folklores
Inker of marvellous verses
"Peace be with you"
To disvirgin my innocence
O evil one

Resting on your canoe of rot
Them suffocates the tempos of freedom songs
Sang in the land of you infiltration
You rascal of sleep!

But still my songs say so, o thief
Call me, Pacifica
E, ocean of love
For my love is not your kind…
But my own roots
So, call me Pacifica
E, ocean of love.

Nationalist

Messing tongue's
Roaring rampaging wind
Barrel for roses

Mr Politician

Belly. Bald mumbo-jumbo
Heap me "X"; sleep and wake "X"
Liar and parasitic
Conman

Cry Bougainville

Cry Boug…weep thy Boug…
For you made slave
On isle of fold reefs
You know no rich living
From this'd land of yours
Throughout oldest ages
But beautiful perfect
Media cover story of perfection
For men far and wide
Ad to come running
To dig in
Deep and deep and deep down

Cry Boug, weep Boug…
For yours realistic pride is
Fading to wrinkled
Ugliness…
Mungkas turns ulungasi
Green skins brown
Hills born flat and barren
Life hugs west
A journey hated by old papa
You'd call sickness
And run away
You stupid naked lunatic

Cry Boug, weep Boug…
This is the same story-snoring,
Though, with good lines-
Worth learning her story silently
O'er and o'er
The game is that gaining
The drill of politics
For my blackness
Labouring long

To fruition folklores
Of the sunset grace
Legends
Anew.

Pacify Solomon

Calm the Cyclone
O celestial race
You'd appraised upon the path
Of my woeful sole…
O gods of pure rage

Ponder the nerves of your chop
And sweep the clouds of annihilation
Over again
Of my weeping children
Burgeoning sandly heads
Grasping and singing
In multitude of dreams
O path to the darkest huts
Of subjugated defeat

Sickle, sickle that storm
In the horizon, o
Gods of hills and caves …
Cool your snooty heartily valves
Blooding my philosophy of oneness
As my doctrine of just mungkas
Is drifting aloof the wisdom

O, hear the cry of the peace maker,
Living dove in the mountains,
Winged, but can't soar
High enough
To lamp the crimsoned land

To historic identity attire

O masters of the spirited,
Gallantic to the cry of Solomon,
You chief of these siblings
That is exiled by your anger
Strike
Behind the bars of strife,
Heal them …

O mystic beings of clouds and seas,
On the seas you dwell
As Solomon
Reaps
The distress of your rejection
That burns the skyline dead

How awful your moods,
Spirited flesh and stars?
O how'd lethal you'd be?
Solomon bleeds; and
Dies in the seas rights,
O scared heart
For you forgot you'd promise
Of mungkas salvation.

O salvation
From relegation

So she'd lost,
Lost she shall be
And look everywhere
By the westerly clouds
That graves
The land plumage
To shameful misery

O celestial race
Rekindle afire
Brotherhood of happy isles
Then, o child
Of heavenly home
May nurse your tune-
A tune of piousity –
In the morning sunshine
Of your spirit world
In the sky azure
And rivers sparkling splashing
That strike strong
With art of listening
Your soil, soul and lustre –
Bleeding panic
By you'd own inspiration

O Solomon
Homage the heavenly creation
That gratifies the bemoaning soul
With endless
Chains of shells and feasting
Amongst waves of blue
And greeny lustre

Dancing from Bougainville to San Cristobal
O cry of liberation
To the celestial kinship
That's anew'd the agony
In ours over
The Solomon archipelago

Calm,
O calm me
From tears of desolation we bear
From ages of slavery
In our land,

Beautiful Solomon
Where'd our umbilical cord
Was teared once upon a time
Quell my tears
O host of spirited ancestors…
Calm this rage
To perfect peace
We'd cry for all

Erereng

Erereng,
They cross the seas in dozens…island hopping!
The Kawas dreaded and hid
Silently secured in heaven of gold.
Of gracious heavens, he wandered…
That was harmonious torrential waters
In the swaying land of Monahe.

For this, the beast
Fights the streets and dry the creeks up
And bit the strangest drums
Scaring far the eyes that see…
And ears that hear
That foreign song of death
Glaring fierce than tearing crocodile.

But this invader; cares not… the law, and
Robs that house beside dreams
Through that window for gold
He fingers the white child
Giving life beyond needed—screaming—hysteria!

To the silent holy night
Cyclone blustering neighbourhood's doubt
So the morning on Bougainville

Sees nothing lovely
But messed up cups, spoons and forks
And run away attire
For that beautiful Sunday morning

That erereng
No oasis in yoking moment
Strolls the street up and down
Looking the whitefella in the face
Pealing dingdong at
That gate of last storm… he knew 'bout

"Laikim wok'a,"he say with fear
Clouds gather…
Hours getting longer and longer
As whitefella laughs: "Me thinking you out."
The sun gets gloomier as he stands
"Cleaner your pikinini pekepeke, okay." He interrupts.
He alas, confesses, to the world
That straying trouble of the Arawa nights.
As whitefella puffs to his ears: "No wok'a. Only skul boy needed"

Wonder tortures him down…
No spoons for the fading hours…
So, belly ringing painfully for a pot of rice;
And cool eyes on the bins,
This wander dog, roams off.
Roams the peaceful nights hour raving his dirt.
Beyond the asphalt laid for the Blackman, he travels
To the black hillocks, he staggers
To peep and rape the motherland.

He loots, fruits of sleepless nights and gobbles.
In heaps, he packs and barrow far… into the streets.
Through the street of the whitefella fella he goes,
Singing: "twenty cents."

O evil axis,
Luckiest one sitting in the air of Panguna
And chases with the rod
Leaching the sanity of the Blackman,
Off this land of his birth…
By the roar of the bulldozers and dynamite,
Mountains of water fade… the Blackman is sick…
O inspirational chats of gods, gone
Gone to land beyond the horizon.

Behind the wheel of cruelty, they cry, as
This beast, in pride, laughs and laughs…
In ties and socks, he gestures love
So sour than lemon, though, to the Blackman,
He dances,
As he sings the sweetest songs
To his new found land
Knocking beside the weeping of the land
To purest servitude

The Blackman heart
Down, from much hopelessness
For waters of living,
Dashes Street to streets—
Doors ajar but rigid—
For thorning,
Til he hits cliffs of no perfections

Standing erect by the outskirts are his nightmares…
Those slums of dirt and death
To the striving local brew: the cry
Of my black women

O beggar,
You black heart
With god's creature pain

And gloomy insanity.
No penny. Leached!
Swaying by the harsh shores and thorny paths
You cry
As the infiltrator crooks
Nest millions in flooding banks
Upon honey of crows that fly south; as you, the
Humbled, teary eyes
die labouring…
O black slaves
Of my beloved Bougainville

Equality

Lovers by ribs
A million joy
Colouring no-arms salvation
Side by side

GLOSSARY OF KIETA WORDS

Bak'a - (expression of joy) oh

Bani'areng ko - (joking) a being with a penis

Barapaang - a clan (Eagle as their totem)

Bi'aang - banana

Bia-ko ameai - give me a share of your beer

Biriko - a traditional fan for dancing, decoration … etc. of the Kieta people

Bompo'ronang - a girl of the Bompo (Millipede as totem) sub-clan

Da aung - you

Dome'na - (Evo) the sun

E're - (plural) hey

Ere'reng kong - a New Guinean. Non-Bougainvillean

Kara - moon

Kavoro - house cook

Kawas - a Bougainvillean referred commonly for being jet black

Kekere'u - edible water frog that makes a lot of noise in its dark chambers

Ko'teu - sweet potato

Koro - yam

Kovi - bamboo flute

Kunu'nava - ceremonial hut where girls are kept after menarche

Kura bang - a clan (the Fresh Water Bass as their totem)

Mungkas - (Buin) black

Nai'namung - day of drinking

Nem'makaa - a young boy

Oii - oh (joyful surprise)

Pakia - crocodile

Piaru - unsuccessful person

Siriroi - traditional singing style (ritualistic)

Sirivi - sweet smelling herb used for grooming for singsings

Sivoi - a small bird with dancing tail

Tamatama - traditional food (pudding) prepared in coconut oil

Te - that

Tora - traditional knapsacking, storage etc… bag

Utau - a traditional clay pot

ABOUT THE AUTHOR

Leonard Fong Roka was born in 1979 in Arawa, then the capital of the North Solomons Province (Bougainville) in Papua New Guinea. He was the first born in the family and has a younger brother and three sisters. His father's traditional home was Bali Island in West New Britain Province, but he never set his foot on his patrimonial land and grew up on Bougainville. He was killed during the 10 year crisis.

Leonard began his schooling at the Piruana Village Tokples School outside Arawa in 1986. In 1987 he attended Peter Lahis Community School on the eastern edge of Arawa untill 1989 when the Bougainville conflict intensified. In 1990 he and his younger brother were transferred to the much-centralized Kaperia community school by their cousin-brother (grandmother's brother), the late Joseph Kabui, who was then Premier of the North Solomons. The classes were halted midway by the PNG blockade on Bougainville. However, the 1994 ceasefire allowed him to re-enrol. He completed Arawa High School in 2000 and graduated from Hutjena Secondary School in 2002 and went to the University of Papua New Guinea in 2003. In 2004 financial difficulties forced him to abandon his studies.

He began writing poetry in 1997 while in Grade 7 at Arawa High School. After leaving university he also began writing short stories and started on a Bougainville Crisis autobiography project called *Brokenville.*

After 7 years out of the education scene, he returned to university and is currently a student at Divine Word University in Madang.

www.ingramcontent.com/pod-product-compliance
Lightning Source LLC
Chambersburg PA
CBHW060804050426
42449CB00008B/1527
* 9 7 8 0 9 8 7 1 3 2 1 4 7 *